ACKNOWLEDGEMENTS

Gia Pampellone, Bill Patterson, Roda, Steve Manning,
Jennifer Bain, Diane Patrick, Wade Hudson, Lonnie Gordon, Dr. Padu,
Faki Shaafi, Judith Solomon, Mama Nyaah, Bill Banks,
Betsy Volante, Kwasi Mensah and Dr. Sebi

Written by Ron Seaborn

Illustrated by Everette Allen and Alex Morris

Colored by Pete Sprankle

Art concept by Ron Seaborn

Art direction by Ron Seaborn

Book designed by
Pamela Kersage, Chassman Graphics, New York City

Dedicated to
Shirley and Sis, with love

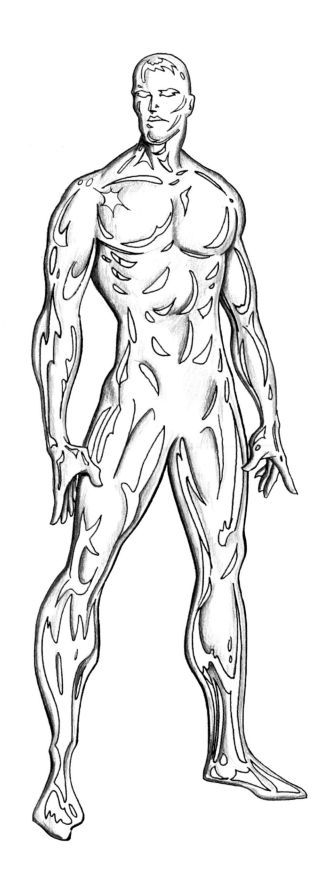

Hi, they call me **GLASS MAN**. I come from New Rock. They call me **GLASS MAN** because you can see through me. My glass body allows you to see when I have eaten the right food and when I have eaten the wrong food.

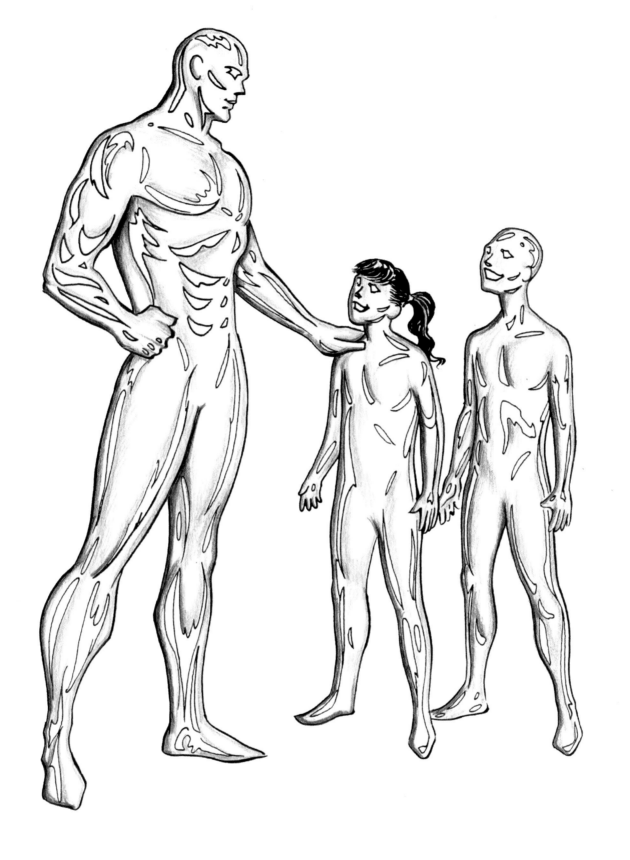

Imagine that this is your body next to mine! Also imagine that your body is made out of glass... just like mine. Now imagine that you have become **GLASS GIRL** or **GLASS BOY.** You will also be able to see when you are eating the right food and when you are eating the wrong food.

Let's go on a journey to explore the world of food. As we go on our journey, we are going to find out what the wrong foods are and what the right foods are. Let us find out why some foods are wrong for us to eat and why some foods are right for us to eat. On this adventure we are going to see **The Meat Monster, The Sugar Demon, The Dairy Goon, The Starch Creature** and **The Mucus Destroyer.**

These dangerous creatures are the **MUCUS GANG**. They are wanted for clogging up the entire body with mucus and making people sick. They are being hunted and tracked down by **THE HEALTH GUARDIANS** who want to keep us healthy. **THE HEALTH GUARDIANS** would like you to help them get rid of these villains so that we all can live a healthy, happy and long life. **THE MUCUS GANG** is wanted all over the world for the damage that they do to our bodies.

WANTED

THE MEAT MONSTER

DEAD OR ALIVE!

For helping to cause cancer of the stomach and the intestinal tract.
For helping to cause ulcers. For over working the digestive system.
For causing uric* acid to attack the muscles of the body, causing us great pain.
For helping to cause heart attacks, poor circulation, high blood pressure,
and committing other crimes against mankind.

*Uric Acid—acid that gets into the muscles and crystallizes like glass.

WANTED

THE SUGAR DEMON

DEAD OR ALIVE!

For causing sugar diabetes. For helping to cause constipation.
For causing children to be irritable and neurotic.
For robbing the body of multi-vitamins.
For helping to destroy our teeth, kidneys,
pancreas, and committing other
crimes against mankind.

WANTED

THE DAIRY GOON

DEAD OR ALIVE!

For attacking the body with lactic acid
in the form of butter, cheese, milk, yogurt, ice cream
and other dairy products. These foods also cause
too much cholesterol to get into the arteries.
For helping to cause high blood pressure,
poor blood circulation and commiting
other crimes against mankind.

WANTED

DEAD OR ALIVE!

For attacking the body with carbonic acid in the form of biscuits,
bread, cakes, cookies, pasta and other processed starches.
These foods also cause the liver to become as hard as a piece of wood.
For causing stones to form in the gall bladder and kidneys.
For causing hemorrhoids, tumors, cancer and
committing other crimes against mankind.

WANTED

DEAD OR ALIVE!

This is the leader of the notorious mucus gang. He is the most dangerous
and most destructive of the gang. He has no mercy or compassion.
He will begin to destroy you the moment he enters your body.
He is responsible for all the pain, suffering and death that
is caused from eating the wrong foods.

These creatures are able to take advantage of us when
we eat and drink traditional breakfast, lunch and dinner meals.

These meals are full of **The Meat Monster, The Sugar Demon, The Dairy Goon, The Starch Creature, and The Mucus Destroyer**. They are our enemies and will make us sick. Let us find out why these meals are not good for us to eat.

At breakfast we eat: Bacon, eggs, cheese,
french toast, pancakes, white bread, cereal, waffles,
and other foods. We also drink milk, coffee, juice and other beverages.

13

At lunch we eat: Big burgers, double burgers, triple burgers, meat sandwiches, cheese sandwiches, peanut butter and jelly sandwiches, french fries, hot dogs, pizza, pastries, pasta, and other foods.

At dinner we eat: steak, pork chops, lamb chops, spare ribs, meat loaf, meat bi-products, soul food, spaghetti & meat balls, white rice, pasta, chicken, fish, pies, cakes, ice cream, and other foods.

There are more foods for each category, but these examples will serve our purpose.

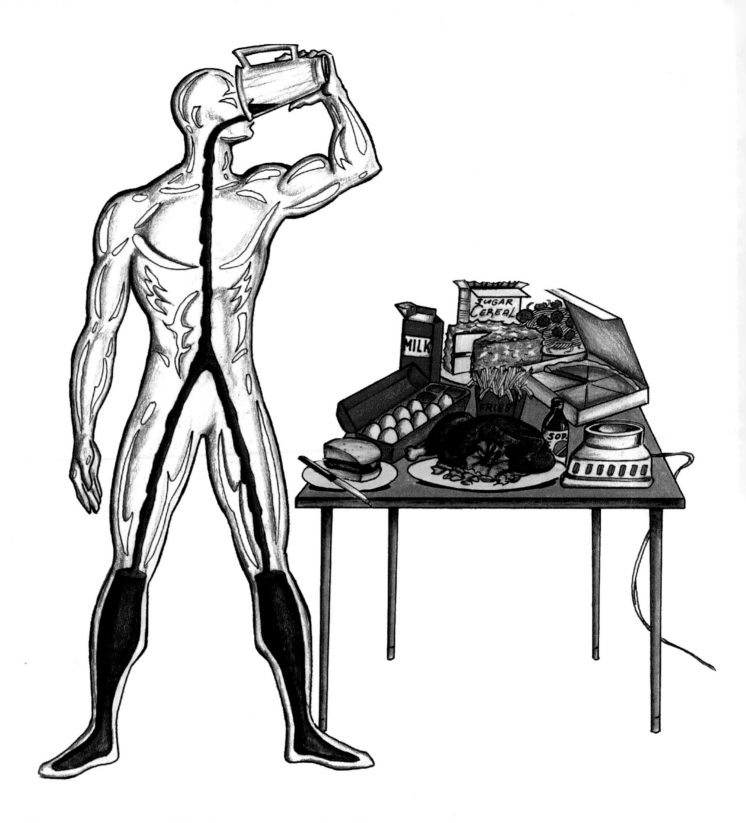

Let us imagine a blender. Imagine this blender is your body. Let us put any
one of the meals we have just read about into the blender along with whatever
we drink with our meal. Let us now imagine the blender is chewing food in
much the same way as we would chew our food. We pour the thick gooey food
into our glass body. The food travels throughout our entire system after the
digestive juices in our stomach breaks the food down.

This is where our troubles begin. This food is like heavy mud traveling throughout the body. This mud begins to clog the body's systems the minute we eat it. This mud is really **MUCUS**. The mucus blocks and clogs the entire body, stopping the blood from fully carrying oxygen to our brain and throughout the rest of our system. Without oxygen reaching our organs, those organs start to break down and we get sick. Our cells cannot breathe and our organs cannot breathe. This mucus, combined with a lack of oxygen, causes heart attacks, high blood pressure, strokes, kidney failure and all of the other diseases that grown-ups get.

By eating this way we age quicker, we gain weight and we look very bad.

Oxygen is the most important element that our bodies need to stay alive. You can live 110 days without food, 16 days without water but only a few minutes without oxygen.

At this point we have eaten only one mucus meal. Now imagine putting two more mucus meals on top of the first meal before the day is over, along with all the junk food and sweets we eat. Now imagine doing that everyday of the week, everyday of the month, everyday of the year. Can you imagine doing that everyday of your life? Can you imagine all of the mucus we will have clogging up our entire system? This mucus is the main reason our bodies change drastically at 50 or 60 years of age and in many cases fall apart.

Do you know people eat differently all over the world! They eat animals that we probably would not eat. In different countries people eat dogs, cats, horses, donkeys, rats, wild animals, lions, tigers, gorillas, monkeys, elephants, reptiles, snakes, lizards, crocodiles, insects, termites, spiders, ants, and other living things they should not eat. They do not think anything is wrong with the way they eat for the same reason that we do not think anything is wrong with the way we eat. They have been eating these animals all of their lives just as we have been eating the animals we eat all of our lives.

We eat cows, pigs, sheep, crabs, lobster, shell fish, possum, rabbit, squirrel, and other living things. All of these creatures are mucus forming and are not meant for human beings to eat. A wise man once said "**DO NOT EAT ANYTHING THAT HAS OR HAD A HEAD ON IT.**"

The mucus gang is responsible for the ailments children have at an early age, such as colds, flu, fever, tonsilitis, belly pain, appendicitis, diarrhea, constipation, worms, eczema, skin troubles, coughs, asthma, runny noses, being overweight and many other ailments. Remember, these problems enter our bodies in the form of candies, cookies, cakes, pies, french fries, potato chips, pizza, hamburgers, eggs, cheese, milk, and many other bad foods we eat. Our blood must flow through our bodies like water, not mud.

THE MUCUS DESTROYER and his gang pull the skin down and makes it sag and look very wrinkled after years of this type of eating. That is why many adults start to look older than they really are.

Just as we grow from a baby into an adult, so does meat, sugar, dairy, and starch change into mucus.

The Mucus Destroyer with the help of his gang is going to make sure that we are miserable and in pain and eventually they will destroy us and send us to an early grave.

While we are young, we are not going to experience most of the problems that adults have from eating the wrong food.

But if our diet remains the same, by the time we become adults we are going to be sick and develop the same problems.

The mucus problem begins when a mother starts to feed her baby cow's milk or any of the other commercial baby formulas. **THINK!** Aren't most babies round and fat with runny noses? This is nature trying to get rid of the mucus through the nose and eyes. Do you have mucus in your eyes when you wake up in the morning? Do you constantly have a cold? Do you cough up phlegm? Well that is also nature's way of helping us get rid of the mucus. Remember, mucus affects every internal organ and every vein and artery in our body.

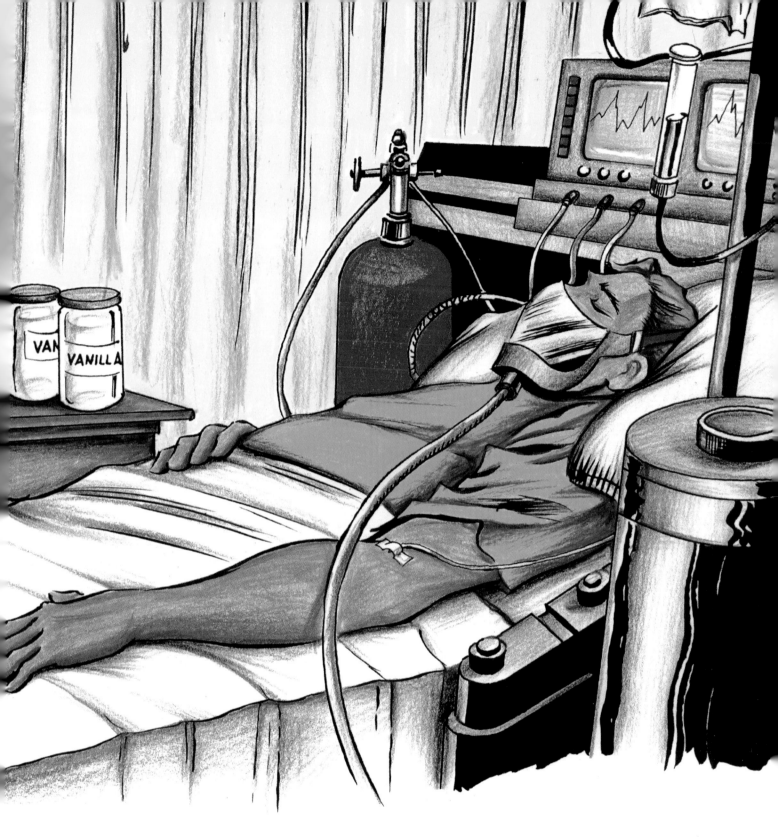

THE MUCUS DESTROYER attacks our body and creates a disease named after the organ that it effects. When mucus attacks the heart, it is called heart disease. When mucus attacks the lungs, it is called lung disease. Why should they call the disease by the name of the organ? There is only one disease, mucus. **How do we eliminate mucus?** We need the help of **THE HEALTH GUARDIANS.**

THE HEALTH GUARDIANS

FRUITARIAN
FIGHTER

GRAIN
CRUSADER

VEGETARIAN WARRIOR

SEAFOOD
GLADIATOR

THE HEALTH GUARDIANS are here to protect our body and keep us healthy and strong. They can only protect us when we eat vegetables, fruits, natural grains and sea vegetables.

You can knock the mucus gang out of your life with the help of
THE HEALTH GUARDIANS.

VICTORY!

Vegetables, fruits, natural grains and sea plants are the best foods for us to eat. They come directly from nature, grown on a tree, a vine, out of the ground or from the sea. Vegetables, fruits, natural grains and sea plants receive the ultra-violet rays from the sun which are necessary to sustain life, energize our bodies and give us strength. Without the sunlight all living things on earth would die. Remember that man-made processed food that comes in a can, a carton or a box is full of mucus. They will fill us up and make us fat but they will not give us the necessary minerals, vitamins or nutrients that we need.

Vegetables, fruits, natural grains and sea plants are light, live, wholesome foods. These foods when digested will easily move through our system, and not wear out our body as heavy foods do. For example, if we were to carry one or two of our friends around on our bicycle, it would break down much quicker because of the extra weight. That is exactly what happens to our bodies when we eat dead, heavy foods.

Whole, live foods contain oxygen, and when we feed our body these foods we automatically become stronger, healthier, feel better and our bodies become resistant to illnesses.

Live wholesome foods also give us the energy and strength we need to become great athletes.

Children who joined **THE MUCUS GANG.**

After they joined **THE HEALTH GUARDIANS**.

GUIDELINE TO UNHEALTHY EATING

THE MUCUS GANG would like you to eat:

Meat or Flesh	All living creatures that walk, swim, crawl or fly including insects.
Starches	Refined white flour, white bread, white rice, refined cereals, biscuits, pasta, pastries, and all other processed starches.
Dairy Products	Milk, ice cream, cheese, eggs, butter and other foods containing dairy products.
Sweeteners	Sugar, commercial honey, artificial syrups, or sweeteners, and all the candy and sweets you want.
Condiments	Salt, black or white pepper, vinegar, and other unnatural relishes.

THE MUCUS GANG would like you to drink:

Coffee, chocolate, commercial teas, carbonated drinks, unnatural fruit drink, and drinks that contain artificial coloring, flavoring, or preservatives, and tap water.

GUIDELINE TO HEALTHY EATING

THE HEALTH GUARDIANS would like you to eat:

Vegetables	All green leafy vegetables, spinach, lettuce, kale, watercress, cabbage, broccoli, zucchini, okras, dandelion, chayote or chrystophene, string beans or peas in pod, bokchoi, mustard greens, amaranth leaves, onions, cucumber, garlic, and other natural vegetables.
Fruits	Apples, bananas, grapes, citrus fruits, pears, apricots, mangoes, figs, cherries, kiwi, persimmons, berries, papayas, and other natural fruits.
Dried Fruits	All unsulphured dried fruits except pineapples and cranberries (too much acid).
Melons	All melons, water melon, cantalope, honeydew, casaba, and other melons of nature. Melons should be eaten separately from other fruits.
Sea Vegetables	Kombu, wakame, arame, hiziki, irish seamoss, dulse, kelp, agar agar, nori and other sea vegetables.
*Natural Grains	Amaranth, quinoa, spelt, kamut, wild rice, teff, and other natural grains.
Sweeteners	Organic maple syrup, natural honey, dates, freshly squeezed fruit juices and other sweeteners made from natural fruits.
Condiments	Cayenne pepper, kelp granules, garlic powder, onion powder, and other natural relishes.

THE HEALTH GUARDIANS would like you to drink:

Water	As much spring or purified water as you can in order to flush the toxins and poisons out of your body.
Other	Herb teas, vegetables and fruit juices from a juicer.

*Natural grains should be soaked overnight or sprouted and eaten raw to avoid the harmful effects of the acid and mucus in them when cooked. A few examples of grains and starches that should be eaten in moderation because of the acid, mucus and starch content are dried beans, cereals, most grains, carrots, potatoes, radishes, turnips, beets, brown rice, tofu, sweet potatoes, cauliflower, nuts, etc. Many of these foods are also hybrid. Hybrid food is man-made food. Man-made food is mucus forming! All **NATURAL FOOD** should be **ORGANIC**. Food that has not been treated with chemicals or pesticides.

ORDER FORM

LIFE LINE, INC.
P.O. BOX 7990
JAF STATION
New York, NY 10116-7990

Website: www.thehealthguardians.com
Email: info@thehealthguardians.com

❑ YES! Please send me **THE HEALTH GUARDIANS** @ $ 29.95

❑ QUANTITY   ❑ FOR A FRIEND

Name _____   Name _____

Address _____   Address _____

City _____State_____Zip_____ City _____State_____Zip_____

Phone # (_____)_____   Phone # (_____)_____

❑ To become a member of **THE HEALTH GUARDIANS FAN CLUB**, please check box!

ORDER FORM

LIFE LINE, INC.
P.O. BOX 7990
JAF STATION
New York, NY 10116-7990

Website: www.thehealthguardians.com
Email: info@thehealthguardians.com

❑ YES! Please send me **THE HEALTH GUARDIANS** @ $ 29.95

❑ QUANTITY   ❑ FOR A FRIEND

Name _____   Name _____

Address _____   Address _____

City _____State_____Zip_____ City _____State_____Zip_____

Phone # (_____)_____   Phone # (_____)_____

❑ To become a member of **THE HEALTH GUARDIANS FAN CLUB**, please check box!